# Getting to **What Matters**

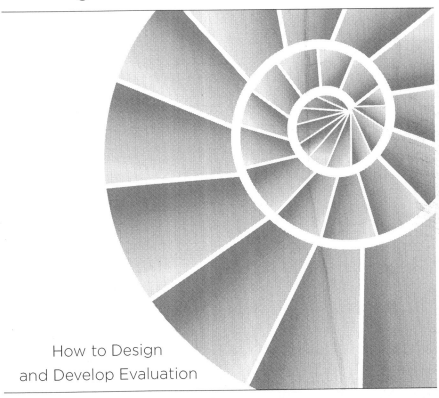

How to Design
and Develop Evaluation

## Steve **Patty, Ph.D.**

Dialogues in Action
408 NW 12th Avenue #506
Portland, OR 97209

**www.DialoguesInAction.com**

*To the many leaders of*

## YMCA's Project Impact

*who have tested these ideas
in thousands of in-depth interviews
throughout North America*

# Table of Contents

# Introduction

Designing evaluation is often drudgery. Administering evaluation is even more painful. We would rather be right in the middle of the action—leading, teaching, creating—than thinking about how to measure our effects or inquire into the qualities of our results. Sometimes evaluation feels just like an afterthought. And who wants to waste time or energy on an afterthought?

But what if evaluation could be more than that?

What if we could actually strengthen our strategy, clarify our aims, develop connoisseurship for subtle but significant features in people, raise leaders, and even improve our ability to draw and engage others in our mission through evaluation?

*Evaluation is leadership.*

What if evaluation could help us see better, think better, focus better, and grow our leaders and our organizations better?

If so, then evaluation would be as much a tool for organizational and leadership development as it would be a duty of reporting, accreditation, compliance, funding, advancement and such. Evaluation would be leadership.

This kind of evaluation would be intriguing and powerful. It would get us to what really matters.

To have this kind of evaluation, we will need to think clearly about evaluation strategy. Here are few points of orientation:

**Evaluation is leadership**. If designed well, evaluation can focus, direct, guide, and shape the future for people and organizations.

**People are the point of evaluation**, and people are complex and mysterious. Even in areas where impact seems untethered to people—the health of a river basin, treatment of animals, property values, innovations in product developments—people are still central characters.

**Simple and elegant is best**. If evaluation is too lengthy or complicated, it won't be joined by those who need it most.

**The story we tell ourselves is just that**. Bias is alive and well in all of us. We will need to be disciplined to see what we don't care to see.

**The process of evaluation should be educative.** The way we approach evaluation should be as formative for people as the findings from evaluation.

**Participation is powerful**. People tend to value what they have helped create and what involves them.

**Evaluation is best when it is iterative**. It should be evolving and developing as our programs and strategy develop.

**Good strategy precedes good evaluation**. If we don't know what impact we intend to have, we will struggle to design clear and effective evaluation.

**Making people critics of themselves is better than making them critics of us**. It helps to ask more questions about what people think of their own development than what they think of our delivery.

**Beware of the naturalistic fallacy**. It is a classic error to define the "ought" by the "is," and to decide what should be measured by what can be measured.

**Evaluation is a human endeavor**. Paying attention to how people make meaning is essential to designing powerful evaluations.

With those thoughts in mind, let's jump in.

# Part 1

## Inquiry

## Introduction to Inquiry

Questions are powerful.

David Cooperrider from Case Western Reserve University once wrote (and I am paraphrasing here), "Every organization grows in the direction of its most persistent inquiries."

This is a critical idea.

It means that the questions you ask, both formally through your practices of evaluation, and informally as you chew on purpose, aim, and strategy in your staff meetings, will actually determine who you will become. Questions will shape you.

*Questions are powerful*

It's important, then, to ask the right questions. It's also important to ask questions the right way. To a great extent, both the kinds of questions you ask and how you ask the questions will form you and determine your future.

So then, how should you inquire?

Let's begin by thinking about the big questions of evaluation.

# The Big Questions, and the Questions Behind the Big Questions

What do you want to know?

If you could know something—anything—to help you be better at what you do and cause greater impact in people you serve, what would you want to know? If something could be known more fully, more deeply, more insightfully—even if it couldn't be known absolutely or completely—what would you want that to be?

At this point, don't worry about *how* you will know, just go ahead and ask the questions you truly would like to ask, even if they seem impossible to answer. Take a moment and jot a few of them down on a piece of paper.

Do you have them?

Good.

Let's take a look at your questions.

Questions of evaluation usually come from one of two intents: (1) to **prove,** and (2) to **improve.**

> *Proving* questions emerge from a desire to see if we are accomplishing what we set out to accomplish with people or situations–if we are, in other words, effecting change. In some form they address the issue, "Are we making a difference, and what kind of difference might that be?"

> *Improving* questions flow from our need to get better at an array of interrelated factors—problems, strategies, policies, approaches, contexts, puzzles, dispositions—in service to the mission of our work. They are usually some form of, "How can we more effectively cause the impact we intend?"

Whether our intent is to prove or to improve, the questions we ask matter. If Cooperrider is right, and all organizations grow in the direction of their most persistent inquiries, then we need to craft our questions carefully. His maxim reminds us: We follow what we look at. We go in the direction of our gaze. We lean down the lines of our constant conversation and questioning. We grow, intentionally or not, in the trajectories of our most relentless curiosity and unblinking attention.

Questions of inquiry usually come from one of two intents: (1) to prove, and (2) to improve.

It's more than just "what gets measured gets done." It's that where we look (and how we look) determines who we become—as individuals, groups of professionals, organizations, and communities. Evaluation forms us.

Take your time, then, and think carefully about the questions you want to ask. Since inquiry shapes the future for you and your organization, evaluating is an act of leadership, or at least it can be.

At this point, don't think about how your questions can be known. We'll worry about that later. Instead, think about what *ought* to be known.

Usually, our first impulse sends us foraging through an array of human puzzles which are helpful to explore before settling on an evaluation strategy. A simple exercise is useful for clarifying them: Start with an initial question or two, then unpack the questions surrounding them—the ones sitting beside, in front of, and most importantly, behind your initial questions. Usually, there is a layer of questions below your initial level of curiosity. These are the "questions behind the questions." Teasing out these "behind" questions is a key step to designing powerful evaluation.

It may occur to you that in our fast-paced, action-oriented, results-driven world, pausing to inquire or ponder about how we inquire uses a reflective muscle that's underdeveloped. We are accustomed to getting things done, not thinking how best to ask about the qualities of our work and the impact we are having among people. But to grow well and with intention, we will need to develop our ability to find and frame key questions.

Sometimes it takes a couple passes to get to the right questions and to get the questions framed right. So then, after you have written your first draft of key questions, go back and re-write them. Constructing a second iteration will be well worth the time.

Remember what you are working toward: If you could know something more clearly, more deeply, or more fully to help you better achieve your intended impact, what would you like to know?

## Worksheet 1.1

### Key questions

What would you like to know in order to see impact and become more effective at causing impact

### The questions behind the questions

What questions would inform the answering of your key questions

# Two Modes of Inquiry

When we go to design evaluation, we usually use two modes: (1) quantitative—to find what the numbers say—and (2) anecdotes—to tell the warmer, human side of our work. You've surely seen annual reports filled with charts and graphs of numbers, sprinkled with stories of lives being changed. And you've certainly heard leaders say, "Our numbers are up (or down), and let me tell you an inspiring (or warning) anecdote to give a human face to the numbers."

Here's what the elements of these two strategies look like:

|  | Option #1 **Quantitative** | Option #2 **Anecdote** |
|---|---|---|
| *Data Source* | Numbers | Stories |
| *Purpose* | Measure | Illustrate |
| *Instrument* | Data Tool | Hearsay |
| *Process* | Standardized | Serendipity or "Treasure Hunt" |
| *Uses* | Compare/Contrast | Inspire/Warn |

The benefits of cool-headed quantitative evaluation (Option #1) are many. Quantitative evaluation can tell us what is going on with the numbers, whether trajectories are rising or falling, where we stand according to our benchmarks, how one division is doing in relation to another, and how we are performing this year in comparison with last. This mode is invaluable when it's done well.

**We know we need another approach to accompany and balance our numbers, and so we usually turn to anecdotes.**

Quantiative evaluation has limitations, however. Not everything of value can be translated to numbers. Albert Einstein once said, "Not everything that counts can be counted, and not everything that can be counted counts." In fact, some of the deepest features of human change are inaccessible to numbers. Key elements of an organization's values, essence, culture, mood, potential, and energy are immeasurable, but *immeasurably* important. This is because qualities are often intangible, nuanced, and subtle. They lie beneath the veneer of numbers and scales. Standardized tools that reduce complexities to a number, a mean, a singular mark of perception are helpful, but not fully adequate to capture or appraise these qualities.

We know we need another approach to accompany and balance our numbers, and so we usually turn to anecdotes.

Anecdotes (Option #2), though commonly used for evaluation, are terribly problematic. Stories are useful to inspire, illustrate, or warn. But in evaluation, stories are notoriously unreliable and misleading. They tend to be selective and unrepresentative. As my research professor in graduate school used to say, "The plural of anecdote is not evidence." A common mistake among leaders is to invoke an anecdote as proof of some result in a population. Many institutional policies are voted into place by way of a well-told anecdote. It's endemic among us all.

We need a different Option #2.

Fortunately, we have another option: qualitative evaluation. Good qualitative evaluation provides a valid and reliable way to go deeply instead of broadly, see qualities instead of quantities, and explore the less tangible, but no less significant features of human and organizational development. It's our true Option #2.

The true Option #2

| | Qualitative |
|---|---|
| *Data Source* | Conversations, Observations, Artifacts |
| *Purpose* | Dive Deep |
| *Instrument* | Human Inquirer |
| *Process* | Organic |
| *Uses* | Discern/Appraise qualities |

Qualitative evaluation has some limitations as well, though. It's difficult to do at scale, and so we have to sample carefully. It relies on humans, and human instruments need to be calibrated just like any instrument. It deals with data that must be interpreted, and the process of analsyis takes concentration and dedication. (To be correct, so does quantitative; but analyzing qualitative data often feels a bit more daunting.) And yet, qualitative is a powerful means of evaluation. It's our true second option.

| Quantitative Evaluation | Quantitative Evaluation | Anecdotes |
|---|---|---|
| Credible | Credible | Sometimes "Incredible" |
| Hard Science | Soft Science | Sometimes "Science Fiction |

To try this for yourself, make two lists: (1) List the indicators of your impact which can be represented by numbers. Then, (2) list all the features that are immeasurably important but can't be counted. This exercise will help you get a feel for the modes of inquiry.

**1.1  Example**

| Quantitative Features | Qualitative Features |
|---|---|
| Number of participants | Maturity of staff |
| Ratio of adults to children | Energy and ethos of team leaders |
| Annual increase in giving | Developing sense of personal agency |
| What we taught | Change in outlook on life |
| Rates of volunteerism | Resilience |
| Satisfaction ratings | Engagement of participants |
| Etc. | Etc. |

## Worksheet 1.2

Describe the key elements of your mission in both quantities and qualities:

| Quantitative Features | Qualitative Features |
| --- | --- |

# Part 2

## Guiding Models

# Introduction to Guiding Models

Any inquiry into the human condition starts with a theory—a theory of what it means to be human.

Our view of human beings determines how we inquire, how we see, how we interpret what we see, and what we ultimately do with what we find. In a way, a theory is like a lens. It draws our attention and sharpens our focus to particular features of human impact.

Our first theory is represented in a model we are calling the *Heart Triangle*. It is a set of ideas about the nature of people.

Our second theory is built on the logic of change—the elements of cause and effect in any program we design to impact people. A theory of change defines the connection between what we *do* and what we seek to *impact* in others by what we do. When we combine the *Heart Triangle* and a theory of change, we have our second model: the *Evaluation Windows*.

These two conceptual models will shape the design of our evaluation and guide our responses to the findings.

Let's jump into them.

Any inquiry into the human condition starts with a theory— a theory of what it means to be human.

23

# Heart Triangle

We have a mission. We intend to make a difference in the lives of people, and through them to influence families, communities, organizations, societies. The desire to do good burns brightly in our hearts.

But what do we mean when we say, "We want to develop people"? What does a *developed* person look like? And what do we mean when we say that we intend to "change society," make "social impact," "improve lives," or even just "make a difference?"

We use words and phrases like this all the time. They are mottos and slogans—a shorthand for talking about our human mission. But do we truly know what we mean?

Getting clear about the basic nature of human beings will help us. We need to know the fundamental make-up of people in order to determine if we are making a difference in their lives. So who exactly are human beings? Where do we look when we inquire into their growth and development, individually or collectively? Let's start with a simple model.

**What does a developed person look like?**

Every human being exhibits at least three capacities: mental capacity (to think, reason, consider, reflect, etc.), emotional capacity (to feel, intuite, sense, desire, etc.), and behavioral capacity (to do, act, react, work, etc.). We sometimes call these the cognitive, affective, and psycho-motor domains. For our discussion, we will use basic terms—know, feel, and do—to address the three primary areas of human capacity and experience. Let's represent these in a triangle.

**Human Being**

**Know** **Feel**

**Do**

Our triangle—like most visual representations about what it means to be human—oversimplifies many complex and mysterious dimensions of humanity. But sometimes the simplest apparatus lends the most usable ideas. For instance:

➢ To grow well, we need to develop in all three dimensions. A person who knows everything but lacks emotional intelligence, for example, still needs to grow.

➢ Each dimension can be a catalyst for change in the others. Growth in one dimension can provoke (but does not guarantee) expansion through the whole of the triangle.

➢ None of these dimensions is the center of the human being. The mind is not the center. Neither are the emotions or the behavior. In this model, development can start at any of the three dimensions and work its way to the others.

We could say, then, that people develop best when they grow in each of the three domains. This means that any program we design to impact people should engage the mind, the emotions, and the behaviors.

This idea may seem elementary, but how often do we assume that if someone just knows something, feels something, or does something, he or she has grown? Some of our programs focus almost exclusively on one aspect and excludes the other two. We aim to teach a concept, or evoke an emotion, or train a skill. But true and lasting human development will exhibit evidence of growth in all three dimensions of the triangle.

In order to avoid the fog of imprecision, it helps to make our definitions even clearer and look at the specific indicators (what we will *see* or *measure* if they know, feel, or do) and the standard or criteria (to what extent it should be exhibited). This provides clarity and protects us from becoming satisfied simply with vague and general impressions of impact.

**KNOW/FEEL/DO**

1. **Indicators**—*specific and measurable (what we will see)*
2. **Criteria**—*the description of standard (to what extent will we see it)*

Here are some examples for an initiative to develop philanthropy:

| Know/Feel/Do | Indicators | Criteria |
|---|---|---|
| Participants will learn about philanthropy (know) | They will be able to state key principles. | 3 reasons for philanthropy 4 traits of a giving organization 2 common pitfalls |
| Participants will feel motivated to participate in philanthropy (feel) | They will have an increased interest in philanthropy by the completion of the initiative | 80% will report a desire to give 60% will report excitement to volunteer |
| Participants will make a decision to take a step of philanthropy (do) | They will indicate a place where they intend to give their time, talent, and treasure. | Within a month of the program, 50% of participants will have contacted a program director |

The impact triangle is helpful, but it is incomplete in its current version. The big limitation is that it might yield only temporal or superficial human impact. Consider this: A person can come to knowledge, yet lack conviction. A person may feel excited, but have no enduring passion or dedication. A person might perform a skill, but never incorporate the skill into an durable habit.

**Development of the heart is difficult to name** Knowing, feeling, and doing, in other words, are not enough. A person's triangle can expand impressively and yet render growth that is still shallow or fleeting.

For authentic and durable human development, the three dimensions of *know, feel,* and *do* need to work their way into the inner person—the person's core, seat of motivation, drive, and center of being. They need to penetrate and take root in the person's heart. (The heart, in our model, is a metaphor for the source of value, affection, motivation, dedication, passion, durability, and will.)

Development of the heart is difficult to name, though. Our terms are insufficient for inner complexities and nuances in humans. But since our model (and our inquiry) needs categories, and labels for those categories, let's try these:

➤ The *heart* version of Know is *Believe*, because knowledge that works its way deeply into a person affects the belief system.

➤ The *heart* version of Feel is *Love*, because a feeling that penetrates the heart of someone influences that person's source of passion, motivation, will, dedication, and the things he or she loves.

➤ The *heart* version of Do is *Become*, because a behavior that takes root in a person defines a sense of identity and shapes a life's trajectory.

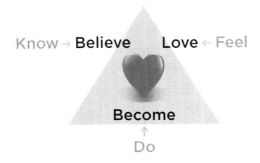

When *knowing, feeling,* and *doing* work their way into the deeper recesses of the heart, when they influence the core elements of someone's being, and when they seep into the enduring essence of a person, we see true and sustaining human impact in *believe, love,* and *become* features. On our more hopeful days, we envision this kind of impact in the whole of the human *Heart Triangle*.

Try your hand at describing the inside-the-triangle ideas for your organization or program. Unlike the outside of the triangle, don't worry about making these concrete or measurable. Work to make them clear, however. You will find that you are using *qualitative* terms to describe these aspects of impact.

Here is an illustration:

**Know** — Know about philanthropy

**Feel** – Feel motivated to participate in philanthropy

**Do** — Take a step of philanthropy

**Believe** – Reshape one's identity to value having a personal contribution in the lives of others

**Love** – Develop a dedication and deep commitment to be constantly "giving back"

**Become** – Grow into a devoted, generous, and charitable ambassador

## Worksheet 2.1

Describe your intended impact using the Heart Triangle:

| Outside-the-Triangle | Know |
| --- | --- |
| | Feel |
| | Do |

| Inside-the-Triangle | Believe |
| --- | --- |
| | Love |
| | Become |

# Evaluation Windows

When we design evaluation, it's tempting to first think about everything we can measure and then design evaluations to capture as much data as possible. We assume that if some data is good, more data must be better. The key question is not about how much data however, but what kind of data? And the only way we can answer that question is to back up and think about the logic behind our intended impact.

Let's make a distinction between what we do (data about our action) and what we seek to achieve in the lives of others as a result of what we do (data about our impact). These are the two primary dimensions of logic underlying our programs.

*We assume that if some data is good, more data must be better*

Logic models are most often comprised of more components than simply Action and Impact. (They usually include Inputs, Activities, Outputs, Outcomes, and Impact.) But basically, a logic model defines the relationship between what we do and the impact of that action among those we serve. It's an "if-then" proposition.

In essence, it looks like this:

| If we do this... | Then we will achieve this... |
|---|---|
| **Action** | **Impact** |
| Program, Intervention, Seminar, Course, etc. | Outcome, Effect, Achievement, Influence, etc. |

Also, we will use our *Heart Triangle* model to distinguish between outside-the-triangle data that are quantitative (know, feel, do) and inside-the-triangle data that are qualitative (believe, love, become). The difference between the inside and outside variables in mental, emotional, and behavioral dimensions of human change is an important distinction.

|  | ACTION | IMPACT |
|---|---|---|
| **Quantitative** | **E1**<br><br>For example: Number of participants in the seminar and what content is covered | **E3**<br><br>For example: Demonstration of new skill learned from the seminar (do) |
| **Qualitative** | **E2**<br><br>For example: Quality of teacher-student engagement during the seminar | **E4**<br><br>For example: Growth in the sense of personal confidence and agency (believe) |

When we integrate the two models, we have four-pane window to bring into view and frame a clear and robust picture of human impact.

The model helps us avoid some common design flaws in evaluation. Watch out for these common errors:

> **Measure E1 and then declare E4.** Quantitative data about our own efforts are easiest to gather and most often right in front of us. Consequently, E1 questions often dominate our evaluation efforts. E1 data are important, but they are about

our performance more than our qualitative impact in others. We need data about E3 and E4 to judge our effect.

➤ **Apply imprecise or one-dimensional thinking to E3**. A common error in evaluation is forgetting that there are three dimensions to the triangle of human impact: mental, emotional, and behavioral. In our attempt to find data that are measurable, we often rely strictly on the feeling dimension (like "satisfaction") or the behavioral dimension (like a demonstration of a new skill). It is good to push ourselves to be clear about the numeric indicators of our effect in each of these three dimensions to gather sufficient E3 data.

➤ **Employ quantitative techniques to assess E2 and E4**. Although a survey instrument, especially one that has open-ended questions, might be designed to dip into E2 and E4 data, we will need a better qualitative strategy to get substantial, inside-the-triangle themes. Trying to get qualitative data from a standard questionnaire is like trying to perform surgery while wearing oven mits.

➤ **Use anecdotes instead of solid qualitative means to evaluate E4**. Anecdotes can be powerfully persuasive but highly unreliable as the primary means to evaluate qualitative impact. Remember, the plural of anecdote is not data.

➤ **Appeal to indirect effects in E3 and E4**. Although we might aspire to lowering crime rates, increasing high school graduation rates, and making the world a more peaceful place as a result of our work, we are appealing to indirect instead of direct effects when we use these as evaluation proxies unless we are working directly with crime prevention, academic support, or an effort to ease global conflict. Our most powerful evaluation will focus on our direct and unique effects.

Before we move on to design evaluation, let's try this. Don't rush this step. As with defining the key questions earlier, our ability to design effective evaluations depends on the clarity of our program's logic, particularly the substance of our intended impact. Most likely, this step will take a few iterations before you have developed the ideas sufficiently. (You'll need more space than this worksheet to develop it well, but this will get you started.)

Below is an illustration of a mentoring program between adults and children. It's not a completed example, but merely a few ideas to get you thinking.

| **Quantitative** | **ACTION** | **IMPACT** |
|---|---|---|
| | **E1** | **E3** |
| | Adult-child ratio | Children knowing more about how to relate to adults (know) |
| | Average number of meetings per month | Children feeling more excited to seek mentoring from adults (feel) |
| | Satisfaction ratings of programs | Children talking to adults more frequently (do) |
| | Variety of activities offered | |
| **Qualitative** | Number of participants | |
| | **E2** | **E4** |
| | Quality of adults | Development of agency and empowerment |
| | Meaningfulness of relationships | Sense of identity and dignity |
| | Kind of connection between adult and child | Vision for "my future story" |
| | Quality of experience of modeling | Resilience |

# Worksheet 2.2

Develop the Evaluation Windows for your program:

|  | ACTION | IMPACT |
|---|---|---|
| **Quantitative** | E1 | E3 |
| know |  |  |
| feel |  |  |
| do |  |  |
| **Qualitative** | E2 | E4 |
| believe |  |  |
| love |  |  |
| become |  |  |

# Part 3

## Qualitative Evaluation

# Introduction to Qualitative Evaluation

We are going to start our design work by considering evaluation that is qualitative. We are leaning into this mode first because most of us in Western culture are biased toward quantitative over qualitative modes. We tend to trust numbers more than other kinds of data. As a consequence, modes of quantitative measurement are often more highly developed than modes of qualitative inquiry. (Just think of how often we use the word "measure" when we talk about evaluating impact.)

Evaluation is a big bucket; it takes two arms to hold evaluation well. Most of us, given our proclivity for numbers, have one "Popeye" arm (quantitative) and one "Olive Oil" arm (qualitative). We need to give special attention to qualitative inquiry, then, if we are to hold a robust and balanced strategy.

**We tend to trust numbers more than other kinds of data**

One important reminder as we begin to talk about qualitative evaluation: We are defining qualitative not by the style of question (for instance, an open-ended question could be either qualitative or quantitative) or by our use of words instead of numbers as data (for instance, if we are doing frequency counts on words either written or spoken, we are still doing quantitative) or by the stories we gather to make a point (remember, anecdotes are not necessarily qualitative).

Rather, we are defining qualitative evaluation as evaluation of a particular *quality* of human development—development inside the *Heart Triangle*.

Our focus, then, is to examine what is happening in the believe-love-become parts of our activity and in the believe-love-become parts of our impact.

Seeing qualities of human experience and human change is what qualitative evaluation is all about. We'll keep our eyes focused there.

# Framing the Qualitative Question

The way evaluation questions are framed determines the architecture of the inquiry. It's important, then, to get the framing right. Let's return to what you want to discover and see if we can frame the question well.

Some frames will lead you to seek numeric data. These questions, and questions like these, will take you toward a quantitative mode:

What are participants doing as a result of the program?

How satisfied are they?

How do people rate this year in comparison with another?

What is the trajectory of our size, scale, level of community saturation or market penetration?

Which key indicators are increasing or decreasing?

These questions will tell you about *what* is happening and *what* is being achieved. What these questions won't tell you is *why*. You may look at the questions above and wonder, "Knowing the answers to those questions is all well and good, but I really want to know *why* people are doing what they are doing, *why* they

GETTING TO WHAT MATTERS

are satisfied to this degree and not another, *why* this program is being received in this way, *why* people are drawn to us (or repelled by us), and *why* the key indicators are tracking as they are." It requires another kind of inquiry, and that leads us to the qualitative mode.

Qualitative questions often look like these:

*What moves partners from connected to committed?*
*How does our culture affect the motivation of our staff members?*
*How does the community uniquely value our presence and role?*
*What is the experience of engagement within our organization or with our clients?*
*How are people being shaped by this program?*

In these questions, we are not looking to compare or contrast, to rank or measure. Rather, we are looking to see, to understand, to discern, and to appraise. It may be helpful to picture any person, organization, problem or opportunity as an iceberg with *what* on the surface and *why* below the surface. In a way, quantitative questions measure the *what*; and qualitative questions inquire into the *why*.

**... you don't have to actually use the word why, but you need to think why.**

When you frame a qualitative question, you don't have to actually use the word *why*, but you need to think *why*. If you are trying to understand better how to see the *why* in people you'll probably frame your qualitative inquiry well.

Bear one caution in mind. When you look at your question, some of you may want to know: "Is X better than Y?" "If we do this instead of that, will we be more likely to achieve our desired outcome?" "Which of our activities will most likely increase the odds of realizing a certain effect?" These are great questions, but a bit more complicated to address directly. They often require experimental or quasi-experimental procedures and need control

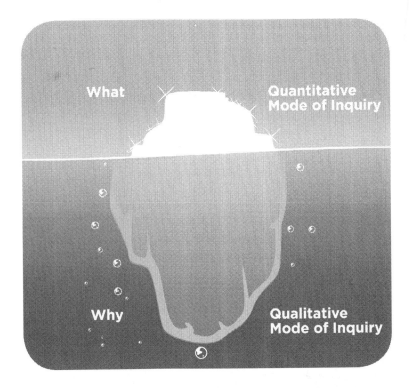

groups and inferential statistics to answer adequately. Apart from having someone on your staff trained in research, you will find it difficult to answer these questions with technical confidence. What you can do, however, is ask the question behind these questions (usually a qualitative one) in order to inform the issue and help you make good decisions about the way forward.

## Worksheet 3.1

Develop a list of five or six qualitative questions as options for your evaluation:

Compose a version of one primary question that will set the direction for your inquiry:

*(For example: How have students grown during this course? How has participation of family members strengthened the family at home? How has our philanthropy initiative developed meaningful volunteerism among members?)*

# Holding a Qualitative Conversation

Not every conversation is created equally. Some just pass the time. Others are animated, but aimless. Still others get us to the heart of the matter, helping us to see more deeply under the surface. These qualitative conversations tend to leave behind a formative nudge.

All of us have conversations. Most of us have many every day. But what makes a conversation qualitative inquiry? Using the *Heart Triangle*, let's craft an intentional conversation to gather qualitative data.

Our aim is to inquire into the deeper dimensions

To focus our task, remember that our aim is to inquire into the deeper dimensions of the human experience. Some people think that "feelings" are at the heart, so they ask, "What have you learned?" And then they follow up with a question, "And how do you *feel* about that?" But feelings are still on the outside, along the fringe in our schema.

Others assume that behaviors are the heart of the matter, and so they ask, "What have you learned, and now what can you *do* in response?" Again, in our schema, a single behavior is on the periphery. When we talk only about knowing, feeling, and doing, we take a spin around the outside of the triangle. We miss the depth we need.

Qualitative conversations requre us to talk about believing, loving, and becoming. But getting to that depth rarely happens accidentally. We need a strategy, a map, a design. We need a sequence too. As you might imagine, it's disorienting and off-putting to dive deeply into the heart of others with no preamble.

Using the *Heart Triangle* as a model, try your hand at developing a sequence of questions, starting from the outside and then going to the inside. Design a conversational pathway (or "protocol") to direct an outside-to-inside interview for each of the three dimensions. Here are some examples to stir your thinking:

### Know ➤ Believe

| | |
|---|---|
| What have you learned in our staff meetings? | How do those lessons shape your perceptions of yourself and your work? How are those making a difference in what you believe to be important? |

### Feel ➤ Love

| | |
|---|---|
| When do you feel most energized/frustrated in your work? | How are you developing your ability to to keep going and stay engaged even through tough times? How have your driving motives and passions changed over time? |

### Do ➤ Become

| | |
|---|---|
| What has been one of your most significant failures this past year? | How has that experience influenced the kind of person you are becoming now? |

With some practice, you'll be able to design a fluid, natural, and elegant interview protocol. Aim for a series of questions that will lead you through a meaningful conversation lasting a half-hour to an hour (usually, about 9 to 12 pairs of outside-to-inside questions). You can begin with whichever dimension makes the most sense. And then you should order your questions to provide a nature flow of conversation and to help people reflect most deeply.

You may be wondering:

➤ *Is this the same as asking open-ended questions?* No. Open-ended questions are usually less directive. You will use the same kind of listening techniques to hear and hold the space for a reply, but you will intentionally guide the conversation's direction (not the answer) to invite a certain quality of reflection and access a specific layer of data. Your aim is informed by the Heart Triangle and Evaluation Windows.

➤ *What if I can't get to anything inside the Heart Triangle?* Sometimes, even the best protocols won't yield a respond from the inside. A shallow answer is still productive data, however. A subject who is unwilling or unable to articulate the core elements of his or her development will tell you something by omission or inability. Finding nothing is often very significant data. Sometimes, the absence of what you expect to hear will be one of the most powerful findings.

➤ *Aren't these "leading" questions?* You are leading the conversation, not asking leading questions. The questions won't lead to a particular answer, just a particular kind of data (that is, inside-the-triangle data). Because of this, you shouldn't try to be detached or disengaged from the conversation. Your job is to listen and gather data, but it is also to lead the conversation to good qualitative data. This requires focus and effort.

➤ *Do I need to follow the protocol rigidly?* The protocol is a guide. You should follow it generally, but not robotically. The aim is to get data from each of the three dimensions and inside the *Heart Triangle*. Your protocol will help you, but you'll probably ask additional questions as the interview unfolds to follow promising leads and press into substantive matters.

➤ *What if we get out of order and the interviewee starts answering later questions first?* Remember your primary aim is to explore the heart of the triangle (and its congruence with the outside). With this schema in mind, you can respond nimbly to the unfolding dynamics of the conversation and keep it pointed toward the right kind of reflection.

## Worksheet 3.2

Design an interview protocol. First develop three pairs of outside-to-in-side questions, then re-order the protocol to flow naturally and smoothly in whatever sequence is best for your subjects.

| | | |
|---|---|---|
| Know | ➤ | Believe |
| Know | ➤ | Believe |
| Know | ➤ | Believe |
| Feel | ➤ | Love |
| Feel | ➤ | Love |
| Feel | ➤ | Love |
| Do | ➤ | Become |
| Do | ➤ | Become |
| Do | ➤ | Become |

# Making Qualitative Observations

Observation can be a powerful means for seeing growth and development in people. Even though we rely heavily on conversations to gather qualitative data, not everyone can reflect on the progress they are making with enough clarity and depth to provide sufficient verbal data for evaluation. In such cases, observations can provide insight where conversations and self-report fail us. But how do we observe in ways that help us see true and meaningful impact?

We need to be focused and disciplined as we look, so that in looking we end up seeing the essential aspects of impact. Otherwise, we will be tempted to pay attention to dimensions in people which are often less about them and more about us. We will get distracted by

> ➤ **what is interesting to me**—looking for what is similar or different about others to me;

> ➤ **what is odd or out of place to me**—watching the unique or intriguing parts in people, that which is unexpected or surprising; and

> **what is useful to me**—seeing only that which affirms what I hope to be true or has utility for my programs and purposes.

*. . . we will be tempted to pay attention to dimensions in people which are often less about them and more about us.*

These aspects of people may be helpful to observe, but they might also keep us from seeing the meaningful features of their growth and development.

The purpose of a qualitative observation is to pay attention to (a) the qualities of participants' current experience and (b) the qualities that are being developed in them as a result of the activity. According to our Evaluation Windows, these categories correspond to E2 – *Quality of Activity* and E4 – *Quality of Impact*.

### Observing E2 - **Quality of Activity**

It is fascinating to observe the qualitative aspects of any activity. An activity is a program, a meeting, an event. An activity is also one person talking to another in the lobby. It is a child leaning forward eagerly in a learning event. It is a group of teenagers lounging casually on the front steps. It is a circle of senior adults drinking coffee, huddled around a table, sharing stories after a fitness class.

To observe an activity, it is helpful to keep two ideas in mind:

1.  There are planned and unplanned aspects to an activity. There is a formal program or curriculum as well as an informal action or interaction that happens in the margins of the activity. Qualities can be seen in all aspects of an activity.

2.  There are both quantitative and qualitative aspects to an activity. Be sure to pay special attention to the qualities.

| Quantities | Qualities |
| --- | --- |
| Number of participants | How they pay attention and interact with the material |
| Ratio of staff to children | What kind of relationships are being developed |
| Amount of questions asked | How their thinking is changing |
| Level of enthusiasm | How they are engaging |

## Observing E4 – Quality of Impact

Seeing qualities of impact takes a bit more attention than seeing qualities of activity. As you might imagine, beyond observing a person over time or having them reflect on their own progress, it is challenging to observe qualitative impact in just a few moments. To observe it in a person, we (a) look for clues that point to the more durable difference that is being caused by the activity and (b) ask those who are in a position to observe over time about what qualities are changing.

While we may not see an entire belief system change, we could see the beginnings of a new way of looking at the self and the world. While we may not see dedication and commitment mature, we could see the initial sparks of passion. While we may not see a clear change in life's trajectory, we could see a glimmer of hope, dream, and purpose. These are signs of qualitative impact.

You'll need to pay attention to the more subtle features of people's behavior and words to get clues as to the kind of qualitative impact they are experiencing. But since we are less concerned about *how much* impact (quantitative) and instead *what kind* of impact (qualitative), you will occasionally see a certain kind of personal confidence, a certain kind of relating to others, a certain kind of agency, a certain kind of caring, a certain kind of energy exhibited through them during the program that will suggest a trajectory of inner develoment as a result of the program.

Also, if it is possible, it will be significant to inquire into the observations of those who are in a position to watch them over time. Ask these observers questions like, "How are participants growing in character? How are they being formed as a result of their involvement? What is taking shape in how they live outside of the program? How are other parts of their lives being changed because of this? What impact appears to be sticking or lasting?" If handled well and analyzed with discipline, this data can be powerful as well.

Remember: we usually pay attention to quantities instead of qualities. Learning to see beyond size, scale, and scope requires us to retrain our eyes. Don't be discouraged if you see nothing related to qualities at first. You will discover these in time, if you keep looking. Keep the ideas of the *Heart Triangle* in mind. You are not just looking for what they know, feel, and do. Your task is to see if there is evidence of deeper development in values (believe), dedication (love), and the formation of habits and ways of living (become).

Here is how to observe:

1. Find an unobtrusive place to watch what is going on. Sometimes it is best to participate in the activity in order not to throw off the social dynamics (this is technically called "participant observation").

2. Pay close attention to what is happening, and how people appear to be doing. There is often much more happening in the subtleties than what initially meets the eye, so stay at it even if it might seem initially unfruitful.

3. Make notes (either mental at first if you are a participant, or in real-time if you are able to position yourself to observe), using both sides of the qualitative portion of the Evaluation Windows in order to keep the two side of qualitative (activity and impact) in front of you.

**Activity** | **Impact**

The more you practice this kind of observation, the more insightful and discerning you will be. You will find yourself not simply thinking about what people are doing, but why they are doing what they are doing and what deeper, more durable changes are taking hold in them. You will develop the same kind of ethnography aptitude that professional researches use to inquire into cultural and social impact. Your findings will be powerful for developing insight into what kind of difference you are making in people's lives.

## Worksheet 3.3

Identify which qualities you intend to pay particular attention to as you observe:

**Qualitative Observation**

| Activity | Impact |
|---|---|

# Analyzing Qualitative Data

There are at least two reasons why qualitative conversations and observations are different from normal, everyday interactions:

1.  We shape the conversation and observation—the focus, sequence, and design—to get data from inside the *Heart Triangle*.

2.  Once we have collected data, we apply rigor to our analysis and intepretation of the data.

Since you now know how to design a protocol and gather data, let's turn our attention to the task of analysis.

For a moment, think about how easy it is to jump to conclusions when we hear something interesting or juicy about someone. We like to make a snap judgment and then suggest a quick fix. We usually haven't much patience to look at the situation twice, let our perceptions simmer, pay attention to nuances and subtleties, or apply discipline to our thinking. We want to run with what we first notice. Contemplation feels like a waste of time, but contemplation is exactly what we need to uncover quality findings which have power and resonance. Insights need time to mature. It takes work to discover texture, meaning, and depth in what we see and hear.

After conducting a few interviews and recording a few observations, you will have thoughts, no doubt. You'll have some hunches about what should *happen*, what should *change*, how this should *affect* the practice of your work. But hold on to your impulse for just a bit. Resist the urge to jump to application as soon as you hear a piece of datum. And certainly, don't make any policy changes right away. Data need to be *analyzed* before they can be truly helpful.

Designing interventions too soon is like throwing solutions at a problem without taking the time to understand the problem, or throwing answers at question before really listening to the question or exploring the "question behind the question." Data need analysis. And analysis requires that you (a) stop to listen inductively to the data (become a "data whisperer") and then (b) look at the data deductively through interpretive frames (become a "lens wearer").

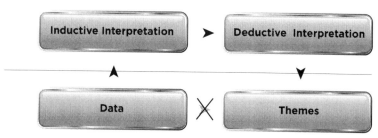

The goal of the *inductive* ("*data whisperer*") step is to hear the data speak for themselves, on their own terms. You have to think inductively about the pieces of the data—particulars, patterns, tones, phrases, postures, etc.—in order to let the true strands of meaning emerge. One straightforward method is to read through the data three times, making notes in three columns—"what," "how," and "why"—and using one question as a lens for each reading. As you move from *what* to *how* and *why*, you will begin to get a clearer sense for the meaning of the data. You will begin to interpret.

> What do you look for? Pay attention to trends, common emphases, pervasive qualities, spectrums, commonalities, differences, relationships, leanings, and the like

The goal of the *deductive* ("*lens wearer*") step is to gain insight by looking at the data through the lens of key theories. In scholarly work, you'll use the literature as the lens to provide insight into the meaning of the data. For our practice, we read the data a fourth time, using our *Heart Triangle* as a lens to look for insights into the believing, loving, and becoming aspects of our human subjects.

What do you look for? Pay attention to trends, common emphases, pervasive qualities, spectrums, causes, differences, relationships, leanings, and the like. Also, look for what is missing, void, absent, and conspicuously or subtly lacking. (Remember, data that is shallow, disappointing, even "boring" can tell you as much as rich and "interesting" data.) All of this analysis will be the material from which themes are made.

The next step is to study your analysis. (At this point look at your columns, not at the raw data.) See if you can spot themes in your analysis. Themes are not always easy to see, but if you analyze the data well and contemplate what you are seeing, you will begin to catch glimpses of pervasive qualities. Picture the ocean's tide receding from the coastal waters at low tide, uncovering rock formations that were previously submerged by a sea of water and waves. The water and waves are your data, your interviews and observations. At first they might appear formless and unending. But those rock formations beneath the waves—structures within the data—are your themes. They will come into view gradually (and sometimes suddenly) as you read and think and rethink the meaning of your analysis. Those formations (or the absence of formations where you would expect them to be) are what you are looking for.

At this point, be careful **not** to

➤ pay attention only to what interests to you,

➤ try and explain what is happening or what you are hearing from your own experience or autobiography (instead, keep asking yourself, "What does the data say?"),

➤ get stuck on the outliers (extreme, exotic, troubling, etc.) instead of the bigger, more pervasive and somtimes subtler issues,

➤ think simply either/or (one of the great gifts of qualitative is that you can have both/and in your themes),

➤ see only what can be seen in a survey (you have come much closer to people than any survey can, so if your themes are sounding like survey conclusions, you're not yet there), and

➤ miss the more subtle nuance and texture in the data (some of your most substantial themes will be subtle, but powerful, because people don't always show on the surface what is most deeply driving them).

## Worksheet 3.4

Use a five column chartlike this to analyze your data. Remember to read through the raw data before each of the first four columns. Then, put the raw data aside and focus on the four columns of your analysis to determine your themes. That way, your analysis will come from your data, and your themes will come from your analysis. (You won't have enough space to write good analysis here; this is only a template.)

| What | How | Why | Heart Triangle | Themes |
|------|-----|-----|----------------|--------|
|      |     |     |                |        |

# Taking Themes to Findings and Recommendations

Up to the point of articulating themes—in all their depth and shades of meaning—you will be bound by the strictures of social science. You will utilize the science-oriented part of your mind. You will hold true to the data in your analysis, and the analysis fin your themes.

But once you have themes, you can begin to think about how to communicate them to your audience for maximum effect. You want your themes to stick with people and influence them. This step is more art than science. It is the step of translating your *themes* into *findings*.

Now, your task is to devise a way to get the message across to your audience. Up to this point, you have been a *connoisseur.* You have been appreciating and appraising the qualities arising from your inquiry. Like a wine connois-

> You want your themes to stick with people and influence them

seur, you've been taking deliberate sips and making disciplined and informed judgments about the qualities you are discovering. But now you have to be a *critic* and communicate your findings in a way that Stanford's Elliot Eisner describes, "lifts the veil of perception" so that others can see what you see.

Naturally, you will need to be clear and straightforward in your presentation (for example, "Here are the four findings emerging from this inquiry, and this is the meaning and substance of each of them"). But you'll need more than a bland rendition if it is to make a difference in people. Try framing your findings in a way that is catchy or surprising. Don't get too fancy and lose the essence of the themes. Just work to make them intriguing, memorable, and resonant.

**You want your themes to stick with people and influence them. This step is more art than a science.**

Your task is to communicate the rich substance of your themes. Remember, you have come closer to your subjects than any survey could, so you can describe features no survey can. Don't forget to talk about the subtle, but significant, textures to the human experience you have witnessed. Help your audience see what you have seen and experience what you have experienced up close. You should be able to offer more than any survey would reveal.

Your findings should be clear and accessible to your reader. But since qualitative inquiry is best suited to access the deeper, more complex qualities of your subjects, you may also find it necessary to include a more nuanced and evocative mode to capture those elements of your findings that are difficult to put into words. This is often accomplished best by using a metaphor. A mental picture has a way of communicating more than words can desribe. In the words of Elliot Eisner, "Metaphor is the arch enemy to the stock response."

Once you have framed your findings, you will need to offer recommendations. Recommendations are your suggestions of next steps for the program or organization. They come from you, the evaluator. They are not a compilation of suggestions from program participants. Here are a few hints to keep in mind as you write recommendations:

1. **Few in number.** Offer a modest number of your recommendations (for example, 3-5 recommendations).

2. **Next steps.** Suggest what would be good next steps along a developmental path. Recommendations can be highly educative if they catch people at their growing edge. As you might imagine, it does no good simply to recommend a perfect end-state. Rather, help people see what to do next in light of the vision for where these steps might lead in the future.

3. **Deeper.** Avoid proposing strictly superficial or tactical recommendations for your inside-the-*Heart Triangle* findings. Remember, if your findings have to do with deeper parts in people, you'll need to offer recommendations to intervene and renovate those deeper issues within people.

4. **Disciplined**. Watch the temptation to insert your personal agenda or pet projects. Your findings should determine your recommendations, not your own intrests and predilections.

5. **Actionable.** Be sure to "close the loop" so that the findings make it to application and don't just sit on a shelf. Place them in a chart of work to make sure they get done. People will need to know who does what and by when.

## Worksheet 3.5

Take your themes, and translate them into an interesting or engaging form. Then identify key points to explain the "meat" of the finding. Remember, you've come much closer to the subjects than any questionnaire could, so make sure that your findings do justice to your data. Keep pushing yourself to explain the depth, subtleties, nuances, particularities, ethos, feel, and essence of the findings. (You will only have space to write a few notes below, but go ahead and begin.)

**Finding #1**

**Finding #2**

**Finding #3**

# Applying Qualitative Inquiry

Getting findings into usable form is challenging but essential if you want your evaluation to make a difference. Getting habits of qualitative inquiry rooted into the ongoing life of an organization, a "way of doing things," is a task even more daunting. But embedding qualitative thinking in people and organizations is powerful and promising for everyone involved. Habits of qualitative inquiry can make a monumental difference in how people approach their work, engage others, and make an impact.

Since most quantitative questionnaires are quicker, more readily scalable, and less demanding than good qualitative evaluation, the odds are stacked against our efforts to introduce, embed, and sustain practices of good qualitative inquiry. How can we increase the likelihood that qualitative ways of thinking and seeing will be adopted?

> Embedding qualitative thinking in people and organizations is powerful and promising

In addition to presenting your research as credibly and engagingly as possible, consider using qualitative models and techniques in other parts of your work. How can qualitative thinking, for instance, be applied to program planning, personnel coaching, organizational positioning, and a variety of other, non-research practices? If you can use the concepts broadly, you will be able to help qualitative thinking take root and grow.

Also, consider what this might look like in your own work. Here are some ideas:

> **Change the conversation.** If you can influence the dialogue, you can influence people. Asking qualitative questions forces people to grapple with issues about essence, beliefs, values, commitments, and such.

> **Keep asking the *why* question.** Don't settle for numbers to tell you how you are doing, regardless of whether they are high or low. Instead, use the numbers as a reason to explore the *why* behind the numbers.

> **Deepen your own thinking.** All people are drawn to meaning. If meaning is highlighted in your own life—your thinking, strategizing, and behaving—you will attract attention. When you become curious about qualities instead of just scale and scope, your curiosity will draw others to similar ways of thinking.

Remember, culture change doesn't happen all at once, for any organization. Growing into qualitative habits, both personally and collectively, is a developmental process. Getting qualitatively fit is like getting physically fit: it happens best through regular practice, discipline, and dedication over time.

Here's a word of caution. Avoid the temptation to use qualitative for the same purposes as quantitative—to compare and contrast, demonstrate scope of impact, or defend size and scale and reach. It is better suited to describing depth, discerning qualities, uncovering the motivations, values, beliefs, essence, and trajectories of growth in people.

Also, be careful not to use qualitative data quantitatively or anecdotally. Resist the urge to do frequency counts on your open-ended questions. (This strategy yields poor qualitative data anyway. Then, simply to count the number of a particular response in an open-ended question is even less helpful for gaining substantive qualitative insight.) Also, resist the impulse simply to gather stories, no matter how compelling the stories. (This sends us on a "treasure hunt" to find a couple of anecdotes for proof of a point we have already decided to make.)

> Resist the urge to do frequency counts on data from your open-ended questions

Qualitative evaluation will illuminate possibilities you have never before seen and open the door to an impact you have never before imagined. The ongoing discipline of qualitative evaluation will deepen and develop the capacity for impact of all those involved.

## Worksheet 3.6

Where in your work, your staff, or your organization should qualitative thinking be applied?

What would be the impact if the people you work with began to see and engage qualitatively?

## Qualative Technical Note A

### Credibility of Qualitative Assessment

In the academies of scholarly research two types prevail, each with rich and varied modes of inquiry and analysis: quantitative and qualitative. Quantitative modes draw on the traditions of mathematics, statistics, and probability. Qualitative modes emerge from ethnography, anthropology, and the humanistic traditions of social science.

Using qualitative research for organizational assessment has been gaining moment in recent years. It is no longer the exclusive purview of academia. Consequently, leaders are becoming more acquainted with using qualitative methodologies and qualitative analysis. Here are a few common questions about this mode of assessment:

### How real is Qualitative Evaluation?

Qualitative assessment, despite the reputation of being the "soft" and "impressionistic" science, is every bit as empirical as quantitative. Empiricism is the back-bone of social science—of any science for that matter. Without the senses, there is no science. The word empiricism comes from the Latin, empiricus, meaning "experience." Qualitative research is rooted in what can be known as we rigorously experience the world around us.

Good qualitative assessment does not just pull its impressions from the air. Findings are based on analysis that is grounded in empirical data we gather conscientiously from human beings. Of course, the data are qualitative in nature, and so they look differently from the "numbers and measures" data of the quantitative type. But they are empirical nonetheless.

In qualitative inquiry, data is gathered from three domains: (1) conversations, (2) observations, and (3) artifacts. These sources of data, when handled with the rigor of good research technique, produce findings that can be as real (if not more so in some cases) as the findings derived from quantitative techniques.

## How reliable is Qualitative Evaluation?

A major methodological challenge of any inquiry is the problem of reliability. Validity has to do with the extent to which the assessment accurately gets at what it is supposed to get at. Reliability is concerned with the trustworthiness of the data gathering, analysis, and interpretation of findings.

Qualitative inquiries rely on disciplined protocols and methodologies that have been developed and established by the social science community. In other words, there are tools, methods, modes, and techniques that have been tested time and again against the rigor of scientific defense. Even though there is often a prominent human (and often artistic) element to the set of techniques, a qualitative assessment that follows the rigor of this methodology will produce findings that are demonstratively reliable and valid and, therefore, credible.

## How convincing is Qualitative Evaluation?

Especially when used in combination with quantitative indices, qualitative findings can be a powerful force for perception, evaluation, and change. Findings are frequently presented in metaphor and imagery and often include representative elements of raw data as heuristics to give texture and deepen insight into the analysis. Findings illuminate subtleties, shades, and nuances that are often below the surface in an organization but end up affecting (sometimes dramatically) organization practice. They explain beliefs, ways of relating, organizational climate, and other elements of profound significance for organizational health and impact.

Certain organizational curiosities are fulfilled best through numerically-oriented quantitative means: financials, trends in participation, and asset capacities, etc. However, other sets of organizational questions are best investigated through qualitative means. Qualitative assessment is uniquely suited to examine issues of social impact, human change, development of belief and value systems in people, organizational culture,

## Qualative Technical Note B

### Hints to Interviewing

Convening a 45 minute, qualitative interview is remarkably challenging, and sometimes thoroughly rewarding. Here are a few hints for how to do it rightly:

➤ Find the right, non-threatening, and non-distracting environment that will be most conducive to authentic conversation.

➤ Think through your introduction carefully before you sit down. Make sure that you get the tone right—enough precision with the right amount of anxiety-diffusing casualness. Address these issues:

1. Thank them for taking time.

2. Speak generally about the nature of your research direction (while taking great care not to lean the trajectory of conversation one way or another). It would be appropriate to say, "We are looking at how people experience their work here," instead of, "We are wondering about the level of commitment of the employees."

3. Make a simple comment about confidentiality so that they know their name will not be attached to any particular piece of information. (Take care not to scare them or be off-putting in your remarks about privacy. You can overdo it and make people think the conversation is clandestine.)

4. Ask them if they wouldn't mind if you took notes.

5. (I usually say something like this, "I want to respect your thoughts and don't want to forget the good things that you say, do you mind if I take notes while we talk?)

6. Then, just double-check to make sure that they are willing to do the interview. (This is our version of a verbal "informed consent.")

➤ Proceed with your interview protocol. If you are doing a single study in teams, you will all use the same basic protocol. Feel free to track down things that interest you, even if they don't belong in the interview protocol as you go. If the same side-issue surfaces in a couple of your conversations, go back and re-work the protocol to intentionally include the issue.

➤ Take notes in a two-column format: the first capturing what they say (both verbally and non-verbally), the second capturing your immediate insights, questions, and commentary as they are talking. (Since you are the instrument, your impressions along the way are also key sources of data.) The first column should be much lengthier than the second.

## Qualative Technical Note C

### Sampling

The biggest challenge of sampling is representation. With whom do you need to talk in order to be able to say something worthwhile in your findings? The size of your sample greatly depends on your research question and the population you intend to investigate. You may find it helpful to narrow your population in order to be able to access a sample significant enough to give your findings power.

As you consider how to achieve representation, it might be helpful to think through the following options

| | |
|---|---|
| Extreme or outlier case sampling | Learning from unusual manifestations of the phenomenon of interest. |
| Intensity sampling | Information-rich cases which are intense, but not extreme. |
| Maximum variation sampling | Document unique or diverse variations emerging in adaptation to different conditions. |
| Homogeneous sampling | Focus on one type to reduce variation and simplify analysis. |
| Typical case sampling | Illustrate or highlight was is normal and average. |
| Critical case sampling | Permits generalization of one important case to others with similar characteristics. |
| Chain sampling | Using the first to identify the second, the second to identify the third, and so on. |
| Criterion sampling | Selecting all cases which meet a particular set of criteria. |
| Theory-based sampling | Finding manifestations of a theoretical construct of interest. |
| Confirming and disconfirming | Selecting cases from those that do and do not exhibit a particular characteristic. |

| | |
|---|---|
| Stratisfied purposeful sampling | Investigating cases drawn from various subgroups within a population. |
| Opportunistic or Emergent | Following leads during fieldwork. |
| Purposeful random sampling | Deliberately choosing a segment of the population to draw from randomly. |

## Qualitative Technical Note D

### Capturing the Data of Qualitative Interviews

Holding a qualitative interview is challenging work. You are balancing a number of demanding tasks simultaneously: trying to be present and engaging with the person you are interviewing, following your interview protocol, probing more deeply into the responses of your interviewee, thinking about how to get inside-the-Heart Triangle, and, of course, recording data. This task of recording data is an essential task to do well. No analysis can make up for poor or incomplete data. So how do you capture them?

If we were doing academic work and seeking to publish our findings in a scholarly journal, we would most likely record and transcribe the interviews word-for-word so that we could code them accurately. For most of us working in the real world however, with management tasks that already exceed the time and energy we have allotted for each day, recording and transcribing takes just too much time and resources.

Instead, to capture data we take notes by hand as the interview unfolds in real time. Then, immediately following the interview, we type them into a document. It takes a little practice. The first few interviews will feel a bit overwhelming. But after you have a couple under your belt, you'll begin to get a knack for it. And you'll probably be surprised by how much data you will be able to capture.

Here are a few hints to keep in mind:

➢ As your interviewee talks, write down as many key words, phrases, sentences as you can. This means that sometimes you are writing as you are looking up at them to make sure you have eye contact along the way. You'll need enough room on your paper for this go well.

➢ Our objective is to capture raw data, just as they are speaking to you. Resist the temptation to summarize or interpret. You'll do that later in analysis. The most valuable data is found in their own words, with their own phrasing and nomenclature. You won't be able to reconstruct this later, and you won't know in the middle of

the interview what will be most valuable to you in analysis, so get this data as accurately and thoroughly as you can.

➤ If they are speaking quickly, and you are missing whole sentences of substance, it's appropriate to ask them to pause for a moment, or repeat what they just said, so that you can get it to paper.

➤ Since people communicate non-verbally as well as through words, draw a vertical line down each page of notes toward the right margin and comment about anything significant communicated by their body language in the margin.

➤ You might have flashes of insight or questions for further thought along the way. Jot them down quickly and circle them to remind you later that those are researcher thoughts and not interviewee data.

➤ Immediately following your interview, be sure to thank them for their time, and then type your notes into a document, back-filling your notes with what you can remember from the conversation. If you do this right away, you will capture an echo of the conversation and will be able to expand your data significantly with aspects you were unable to capture in the moment. The key to hearing this echo is to re-write your notes immediately. If you wait even a few hours, the echo will be lost. (If you are doing the interview by computer technology or via phone and you are typing notes as you talk, go back and fill in what you didn't have time to write immediately following your interview.)

➤ Aim for what qualitative researchers call "thick" data. Tune your ear to listen particularly close to data emerging from inside the Heart Triangle (i.e., what your interviewee believes, loves, and is becoming). This will give you a depth of data, a kind of "thickness," instead of simply a lengthy and thin description of what they say. Good qualitative data will be coming from inside the Heart Triangle, and so be sure to capture this "thick" data. It will be invaluable later and will give you a great platform for analysis.

## Qualative Technical Note E

### Validity and Reliability

As you know by now, qualitative inquiry relies on three sources of data: (1) interviews, (2) observations, and (3) artifacts. Basically, it draws on what you hear from people, what you observe in people, and the intriguing trails of impact (even in other people) that people leave behind. So what makes it special? What makes the qualitative inquirer a more credible source for insight than the normal person who talks to people, and watches people, and pays attention to the surroundings?

The issue is one of confidence. (I am using "confidence" in a technical way here, denoting the measure of certainty that professionals, peers, and constituencies confer upon the results of a study.) So how do you inquire in such a way as to increase confidence in your findings?

Two questions face you. Two big, burly questions stalk the venue of inquiry, requiring the findings you present to be something more than just personal opinion, autobiographical projection, or careless reaction. Those two figures to which you must give account are validity and reliability.

Validity refers to the issue of whether or not you are really "getting at" what you purport to study. To what extent do your design, your interview protocol, your sample, and the other components of your research make scientific sense for answering your primary Research Question? For example, trying to determine how effective an educational program is by asking how much students enjoy the process lacks validity. (The assumption would have to be proven: student pleasure is tantamount to student learning.)

Reliability refers to the consistency of the data over time, in various circumstances, and through different methodologies. In other words, it asks if what you see and hear in this setting is an authentic expression of what is most real. Or, are your data skewed by some ancillary circumstance, pressure, mood, or situation? For instance, to inquire into the life-changing nature of a youth program at a summer camp by asking for a self-report right in the middle of group hugs on the

last day of camp would give you an unreliable data set. (For a variety of reasons, everyone will say, "Yeah, this is the best.")

In order to increase credibility by attending to validity and reliability, qualitative researchers employ the following methods:

➤ **Triangulation**—Taking multiple angles, modes, and "reads" on the same phenomenon (e.g., observe and interview, interview at different points in time, interview a number of people about a particular program or experience, etc.)

➤ **Sampling** — Identifying intentionally rich, diverse, substantive, and meaningful participants that represent the population and, therefore, increase the power of generalizability and transferability.

➤ **Reflexivity**—Caring for the researcher's personal biases that emerge from value systems, history, prior knowledge, moods, etc. (and sometimes double-checking interpretations with interviewees.)

➤ **"Thick" descriptions**—Rich collection of data that is heavily informed by the values of theory (as opposed to lengthy, "thin" descriptions).

➤ **Sensitizing concepts**—Deliberately "pre-heating" the inquiry with particular concepts, frames, and perspectives that will illuminate findings in a certain direction and of a certain kind.

➤ **Convergence**-Organizing the inquiry around a particular question of organizational importance.

## Qualative Technical Note F

### Connoisseurship

One very helpful way to think about qualitative evaluation is to imagine what it takes to become an effective connoisseur and critic of something—art, wine, literature, etc. A professor emeritus from Stanford University, Elliot Eisner, has written persuasively about this metaphor. Here are a few selections:

Excerpts from Eisner, Elliot W. 1985. *The Educational Imagination.* New York: MacMillan.

Another form of qualitative inquiry is found in the work of those who inquire into the work of artists, namely the art critics. The art critic finds himself or herself with the difficult task or rendering the essentially ineffable qualities constituting works or art into a language that will help others perceive the work more deeply. In this sense, the critic's task is to function as a midwife to perceptions, to so talk about the qualities constituting the work of art that others, lacking the critic's connoisseurship, will be able to perceive the work more comprehensively. "The end of criticism," wrote Dewey, "is the reeducation of the perception of the work of art." The critic's task in this view is not primarily the issuance of judgment but rather the difficult task of "lifting the veils that keep the eyes from seeing." (p. 217)

Effective criticism, within the arts or in education, is not an act independent of the powers of perception. The ability to see, to perceive what is subtle, complex, and important, is its first necessary condition. The act of knowledgeable perception is, in the arts, referred to as connoisseurship. To be a connoisseur is to know how to look, to see, and to appreciate. Connoisseurship, generally defined, is the art of appreciation. It is essential to criticism because without the ability to perceive what is subtle and important, criticism is likely to be superficial or even empty. The major distinction between connoisseurship and criticism is this: connoisseurship is the art of appreciation; criticism is the art of disclosure. Connoisseurship is a private act; it consists of recognized and appreciating the qualities of a particular, but it does not require either a public judgment or a public description of those qualities. The perception and appreciation of a particular require a sensory memory. For example, if one is to develop

connoisseurship of wine, one must drink a great deal of wine, learn how to attend to its qualities, and be able to recall from one's gustatory memory—and in the case of wine, the olfactory and visual memories also come into play—the qualities of other wines in order to have a backdrop against which the particular qualities of the wine being tasted can be compared and contrasted.... (p. 219)

In saying that experience counts in the development of connoisseurship, whether in education or in the fine arts, it is important to recognize that the length of time spent n a classroom or the number of museums visited or the frequency with which one attends sports events is not necessarily an indication of the level of connoisseurship someone has achieved. Let us distinguish between recognition and perception, and let us agree with Dewey that recognition is perception aborted: looking is engaged simply to be able to see enough to classify.... If one looks within a classroom primarily to recognize rather than to see, the number of years one spends in a classroom will contribute little to the development of connoisseurship. To develop connoisseurship one must have a desire to perceive subtleties, to become a student of human behavior, to focus ones' perception. Looking is a necessary condition, but looking is essentially a task one undertakes; it is seeing that is an achievement. (p. 220)

## Qualative Technical Note G

### Commonly Mistaken for Qualitative

In the field of qualitative evaluation, there is much of standard practice that goes for qualitative, and may be valuable for you to use at some point, but which is still less than good qualitative. Remember, we are aiming for a certain level of qualities within a person or organization for qualitative. We intended to interact with inside-the-triangle data. Here are a few common practices mistaken for qualitative:

### Feeling Questions

*"I feel satisfied with my experience with this program."*    1  2  3  4  5

Remember, feeling is on the outside of the Heart Triangle. Feelings are helpful to talk about as leads or cues to what might be going on deeper within people. Don't be satisfied with measuring feelings. Qualitative is about much more.

### Reporting Questions

*"I am more confident now after this program."*          1  2  3  4  5

*"I now have a relationship with an adult."*                          Yes/No

Again, this data may be good to get, but it has yet to help us understand the quality of the confidence, and what about the program developed confidence. Neither does it help us see the quality of the relationship with an adult, only that it is there.

### Open-ended Questions

*"What did you like/dislike about our programs?"*

*"How could your experience be improved?*

These are common evaluation questions, but they don't often get past superficial features of the program, and they tend to make participants critics of you and your staff instead of themselves and their own growth and development. Feel free to ask these questions, but be sure to press into E4 questions.

### Story Gathering and Telling

*"Tell me about a time when you were most energized at your job."*

This is an interesting direction of evaluation, but tends to gather anecdotes instead of good qualitative data. This is a good outside-the-triangle question that will need to be pursued further inside the triangle.

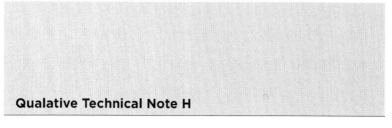

## Qualative Technical Note H

### The Qualitative Process

To help you visualize the process and see the steps, here is a simple diagram of the process of qualitative evaluation:

**Int. 2**
→ "lens-wearer"

Themes → Findings → Recommendations

# Part 4

## Quantitative Evaluation

# Introduction to Quantitative Evaluation

Let's turn our attention now to quantitative evaluation. Remember, unlike qualitative, the purpose of quantitative inquiry is to measure. The data come to us in numbers (or need to be transposed to numbrs) and the application is to compare and contrast.

Remember, also, that we are now thinking about the outside of the *Heart Triangle* and gathering data about what people know, do, and feel.

Measuring the right elements of your work's effects in those you serve can be powerfully persuasive. If you are doing evaluation to *prove*, people tend to trust numbers. A clear and crisp display of numbers can be quite convincing.

**A clear and crisp display of numbers can be quite convincing**

And if you are seeking to *improve*, numbers can give you a sober perspective on aspects of your program you might otherwise overlook. Numbers tend to fix errant assumptions and debunk the cherished theories that compromise our strategies.

A common error in quantitative evaluation is to count all the things you do (outputs), and then declare achievement (outcomes). We need to measure what we do, certainly. But we also need to give particular attention to measuring the outcomes of our work in the people we serve.

How do we design clear and meaningful evaluation that is quantitative? Let's explore the fundamentals.

# Quantitative Design

Where do you start when you set out to design evaluation that is quantitative?

You probably have some ideas right now about what you can count. Maybe you have a list:

➤ Number of participants

➤ Satisfaction scores of staff members

➤ Frequency of a responses from a questionnaire about "take-aways"

➤ Increase or decrease in the number of contacts, members, or volunteers

➤ Statistics of various kinds

Before we continue our list, let's examine at least two tendencies that lead us astray:

1.  **Starting with what can be measured instead of what ought to be measured**. It's not too difficult to find things to count and measure. Some researches will argue that

there is a numeric indicator out there for just about anything related to the human experience. Whether or not
that's possible, we should think about what we ought to
measure before we make a list of what we can measure.
Let's start with what *should* be counted and then move
backwards to indicators and reliable proxies that *can* be
counted.

2.  **Seeking secondary instead of primary indicators**. We
    can also get excited about indirect instead of direct evi-
    dence of our impact. Some indirect indicators might be
    worth measuring. But before we declare that we are go-
    ing to change high school graduation rates, poverty levels,
    political discourse, public opinion, or community well-
    being, we should be clear about our intended direct effect.
    People tend to want to change everything. I call this the
    "world peace" effect. We want our impact to be enormous,
    but to design evaluation we need to decide what particular
    part of the big vision will be our responsibility. Something
    like "world peace" is a wonderful vision, but less helpful
    for the design of evaluation than identifying our unique
    intended impact.

Let's think strategically, then, about the two frames (E1 and
E3) of quantitative evaluation. Below are some questions to help
us. (Remember, we are not assuming that more is better. We are
simply seeking the key indicators or reliable proxies. Whenever possible, consult the scholarship in your field to inform your
choice of which indicators you choose to measure.)

## Quantitative Indicators

**E1 - Effort**

What are the key indicators of your performance?

What about your activity might be tempted to overlook or misperceive if you don't have numbers to help you?

What kind of data do you need to keep you and your team performing well?

**E3 - Impact**

What are the direct indicators of your intended impact?

What are reliable proxies of outcomes?

What are the unique parts of knowing, doing, and feeling in others that you and your team intend to develop?

What needs to increase or decrease in others for you to fulfill your mission?

## Worksheet 4.1

### Quantitative Indicators

**E1 – Effort**

What are the key indicators of your performance?

What about your activity might be tempted to overlook or misperceive if you don't have numbers to help you?

What kind of data do you need to keep you and your team performing well?

**E3 – Impact**

What are the direct indicators of your intended impact?

What are reliable proxies of your outcome?

What are the unique parts of knowing, doing, and feeling in others that you and your team intend to develop?

What needs to increase or decrease in others for you to fulfill your mission?

# Developing an Instrument

Once we have an idea of the key E1 and E3 indicators, our next step is to design an instrument to gather data.

Some data can be gathered without actually inquiring of participants (for instance, statistics from government agencies, research from scholarship in your sector, etc.). Other data can be obtained through standard reporting protocols for program outcomes (for instance, days employed and salary for graduates of a job-training program, rates of recidivism for a juvenile criminal justice program, time in independent living for mentally ill in a day treatment plan).

Quite often, however, we will need to design an instrument to administer to program participants. Here are some hints to keep in mind when creating a questionnaire:

➤ Make sure to balance E1 (activity questions) with E3 (outcome questions).

It's tempting to ask questions about how we did offering the program (for example, "Did you like the speaker?" "How were accommodations?" "Did we keep you interested?") instead of outcome and impact questions (for example, "What did you learn?" "How many new skills can you demonstrate?" "How has your appreciation for this topic changed?").

➤ Ask questions in all three human domains (know, feel, do).

If you are seeking to demonstrate a robust human impact, make sure you ask questions in each of the three primary domains of human capacity.

➤ Whenever possible, provide specifics for the scaled items (instead of pure Likert-style).

Instead of asking a question like, "How physically active are you?" accompanied by a 1 to 5 scale (not active to very active), ask something like, "How many times a week do you exercise for more than a half-hour?" accompanied by a scale (1 to 5 times or more). Providing definition to the scale greatly increases reliability in the responses.

➤ Be careful to use terms that are clear, precise, and easy to understand.

You certainly don't want there to be any confusion in the mind of your respondent. Take great care to avoid vagaries. Every term used in the question should be clear. If a quantitative item can be interpreted various ways, discard it.

➤ Use one idea per question.

In order to get a valid response, make certain that each question has only one idea (avoid the "double-barreled" question). Examine each of your questions to see if there might be a way the respondent will reference one aspect of the question instead of the whole question.

➤ Keep the questions focused on genuine inquiry instead of testing for the "right answer."

Questions with answers showing social desirability or an inferred social bias might skew the data, making respondents answer in a way they think they "ought" to answer or give a contrarian answer to assert their independence.

➤ Use retrospectives to measure changes (or pretest/posttest when you can).

Retrospectives are useful when you can't do an actual pretest and posttest. ("Before the course I was here, and now I am here.") This technique has actually been found to be more reliable than pretest/posttest in situations where subjects might over-estimate their knowledge or skill-level prior to an intervention. People don't know what they don't know, and they often have an inflated view of their understanding prior to learning.

➤ Consider what you might use for a control group.

Apart from doing scholarly work, this is challenging to pull off. A control group is still the gold standard in research. Consider what you might use to demonstrate a comparison between those who have been in your program, and those who have not. Are there ways of getting comparison data from a similar population? Is there scholarly research about your target population that you can use for a comparison?

➤ Pilot your instrument before you use it.

Have a small group from your target population try it out. Then, debrief them by asking: (1) In your own words, what do you think each question is asking? (2) Why did you choose a particular answer over others? Sometimes you will modify the wording or syntax of a question to make it appropriately sensitive. A change of one word can dramatically affect the response.

➤ Pay attention to sequence, organization, and length.

Like any natural conversation, your questionnaire should go from general to specific, non-threatening to more substantial. Questions of similar topics should be grouped together (except in the case of purposeful triangulation). Avoid causing question fatigue. We each know what it feels like to be profoundly bored and bothered by a lengthy test.

➤ Keep it simple.

Remember. Keep it simple.

## Worksheet 4.2

Develop items for your questionnaire:

E1 Items

E3 Items (remember to query know, feel, and do)

# Quantitative Data Analysis and Presentation

You may have heard the saying, "Numbers don't lie." But they do, all the time. Or, at least, our assumptions about what the numbers mean can lie.

Think about the possible ways we can be misled by numbers:

➤ Numbers on a pretest/posttest may not have changed, but it could be that the respondents didn't adequately understand the topic to be able to make a valid judgment on the pretest.

➤ Numbers might have increased over the course of a program, but not enough to be significant.

➤ Numbers could be higher after an intervention, but for different reasons than we think (see Hawthorne Effect and John Henry Effect in the section on Technical Notes).

➤ Numbers might be missing the true brilliance of the work's impact.

➤ Numbers might be inflated or deflated due to influences the instrument cannot detect or external to the program.

➤ Numbers could be lagging indicators of what has already gone by, not what is present.

Most challengingly, numbers often tell us something is happening, but not necessarily why.

There might be a variety of explanations for the numbers as well. That's why it's good to design some qualitative evaluation to accompany your numbers.

Since we are not designing sophisticated experimental or quasi-experimental research for most of our evaluations, we have to be thoughtful as we approach analysis of the data:

➤ Might there be rival explanations for these numbers?

➤ Just because there is a change in the numbers, are we sure the change is significant?

➤ How might outliers be influencing the mean in the numbers?

➤ Could there be a sampling bias? Did we either administer the test to everyone or a representative sample?

➤ Could circumstances or environmental factors skew the numbers?

➤ Might there be hidden motives or social pressures making people respond a certain way?

In more scholarly and rigorous work, there are statistical procedures that will answer many of these questions for us. But for the purposes of most do-it-yourself evaluations, we will simply need to think through these issues carefully and logically.

Also, keep in mind a common bias toward assuming a larger number is better than a lesser number. It could be that an exceedingly high score on an item like "friendliness" might actually belie rigor or accountability. Or, consider how an item like "satisfaction" might actually mean that people are being entertained and comfortable instead of challenged to grow.

After you have thought about which of your numbers are most important and what they might mean, you'll need to communicate them. And since the primary uses of quantitative is to compare and contrast, two kinds of representations seem to be most helpful:

1. **Charts and graphs**

   We won't belabor this point. Just be sure to provide clear and simple visuals emphasizing the comparative relationships represented by the numbers and you'll be fine with this one.

2. **Dashboards**

   Leaders have found benefit in being able to gain a crisp and clear visual of the primary quantitative indicators of performance (E1) and outcome (E3). The key to designing a good dashboard is to identify only a few critical indicators, refresh the data frequently, and find a way to visually represent them on a single page.

Even though numbers, charts, graphs, and dashboards seem to be self-evident, you will need to discuss quantitative findings in a brief narrative to help your audience understand the significance of what you have found through the numbers. This is an important leadership step in all evaluation—helping people to see the meaning and significance of the data.

## Worksheet 4.3

What kind of visual representation of your data would be most helpful to present your quantitative findings?

What 5 or 6 key indicators would be essential to include on a performance dashboard?

# Determining Findings and Recommendations

Wise and insightful conclusions are not always self-evident, even from well-displayed numbers. People can see numbers and fail to grasp their significance. Our job is to unpack the meaning of findings and propose recommendations.

Evaluators often want to skip this part of the work, but this a responsibility of leadership. It should not be missed.

There are a few common errors when approaching this task:

### Error 1

**Taking suggestions from participants as recommendations.** Picture yourself asking for recommendations from new recruits at a Marine boot camp. You can imagine the kinds of suggestions you'd hear: "Less exercise, more sleep, better food, and less yelling please." The data will tell you something, but the data need interpretation before valid conclusions and implications can be generated.

### Error 2

**Assuming that high rates of happiness or satisfaction among participants is good.**

The speaker might have been entertaining and the training filled with interesting activity. Everyone might have enjoyed themselves immensely. And yet no clear and durable impact is made. As Jean Piaget reminds us, "Disequilibration is the engine of growth." If he is right, then "satisfaction" might not be the most reliable indicator of development after all.

### Error 3

**Assuming there is inherent value in the numbers.**

What does a score of 82 on a staff satisfaction mean anyway? It has to be given interpretation or its meaning is empty. As we have established, an exceedingly high number on a trait that we consider positive (for instance, leadership vision) might bode ill for the presence of other complementary traits we also value (for instance, leadership collaboration). The same is true for lower numbers on undesirable traits.

### Error 4

**Using frequency counts on open-ended questions as a substitute for qualitative.**

It is fully appropriate to treat open-ended questions in your instrument quantitatively. There is benefit to counting the number of times subjects give a particular response and showing the array of possibilities, along with the percentages in the categories. This is helpful as a quantitative approach. Just be sure not to assume that it is qualitative.

The part of evaluation we call "Findings" is the part where we say, "Here's what these numbers mean." This is usually followed by "Recommendations" which is where we say, "Here's how we should respond."

**Findings.**

Discuss the most significant features of the numbers. Connect them to the meaning and mission of your work. Use them to prove more sufficiently and to improve more diligently.

**Recommendations.**

Offer only a few recommendations from your analysis of the data that hold the most promise for making a significant difference in your effectiveness. As with qualitative recommendations, be careful not to simply recommend a "fixed" or "perfect" state (for example, "We recommend that we need to reach and impact everyone perfectly") and instead recommend the next few steps (for example, "We recommend that we need to improve our points of access to underprivileged in our city's core.")

## Worksheet 4.4

Even though the charts, graphs, and dashboards might seem self-evident, you will need to provide some narrative to explain the meaning and significance of the numbers and then to provide some next steps. This is an exercise of leadership—helping people see the right things and know what to do with what they see.

Significance of the numbers:

Recommendations:

## Quantitative Technical Note A

**Here are some common types of questions you may consider using:**

Likert-style questions    Strongly agree to strongly disagree along a 5 or 7-pt scale (many more options and you lose reliability because the scale means different things to different people).

Example
*I am now more confident in my ability to design evaluations.*

| Strongly Disagree | | | Strongly Agree | |
|---|---|---|---|---|
| 1 | 2 | 3 | 4 | 5 |

Scaled questions    A numeric gauge in which you provide the specific numbers in the items.

Examples:

**CES-D Scale (Center for Epidemiological Studies, National Institute of Mental Health)**

Rarely or none of the time (Less than 1 Day)
Some or a little of the time (1-2 Days)
Occasionally or a Moderate Amount of Time (3-4 Days)
Most or all of the Time (5-7 Days)

**Policy Advocacy Behavior Scale**
Our agency testified at ___ public hearings held by city council.

| 1-2 | 3-4 | 5-6 | More than 6 |
|---|---|---|---|

| | |
|---|---|
| Binary questions | Agree/Disagree or Yes/No |
| | Example: |
| | *Have you decided to become a volunteer?* |
| | Yes   No |

---

| | |
|---|---|
| Write-in questions | Questions which require the respondent to provide an answer and with which you will do frequency counts throughout the data corpus |
| | Example: |
| | *In what areas of your work do you intend to apply this course material?* |

## Quantitative Technical Note B

Common mistakes to avoid:

### Questions which are too complex

"If you could give advice to your management team, but you had to work within current budgetary constraints and remain true to the guiding values of our organization, what would be the most significant change you would suggest?"

### Questions that are vague

"How would you rate your life?"

### Questions with multiple interpretations

"Do you consider yourself a spiritual person?"

### Questions with multiple ideas

"Do you want to be rich and famous?" "Have you ever been called names and had your life threatened?"

### Questions with a built-in social bias (or social desirability)

"Do you usually care about doing good work at your job?"

### Questions that lead

"With all of the hunger in the world, do you really think it is fair to waste food?"

### Questions relying more on perception than reporting (unless perception is the nature of the research)

"Will this training help you reduce absenteeism among your staff?"

### Questions primarily about satisfaction

"How satisfied are you with this conference?"

### Questions with multiple (and limited) choices unless you are certain you have an exhaustive list of the right choices (often defined by scholarship or previous research).

"Would you say that your style of leadership is more like a (a) pioneer, (b) entrepreneur, (c) manager, or (d) inspirer?"

### Questions for the sake of affirmation

"What do you think about our generous gift to your organization?"

## Quantitative Technical Note C

### What to do with numbers

We are not going to perform much more than the basics of descriptive statistics and measures of central tendency in most cases. Here are a few common examples:

#### Mean

A mean is the average. We use it when we want to get a general sense of how our people are doing.

For example: *"Prior to our training program, participants reported a confidence level of 2.7 on a 5-pt scale. After the program, the self-report mean was 4.2.")*

#### Median

When you suspect that there will be outliers that will skew the average substantially and make the mean misleading for people, use the median. The median is the point midway through the line-up of responses if you were to place them from lowest to highest, or highest to lowest. Sometimes, when there are a few extreme cases in our data, a median will give us a clearer picture than a mean.

For example: *"The median annual contribution from our board of directors is $8,400.00" (One board member donated $50k, but most of them gave between $4k and $12k.)*

#### Mode

Sometimes we are interested in identifying which answer was given most often. This is the mode. It is the response most "popular."

For example: *"More attendees rated this seminar as the best than any other."*

#### Frequency Counts

We perform frequency counts on either closed questions (multiple choice) or write-in questions to get a picture of relative strength of responses across the spectrum. The process is simple: just add up the number of same responses.

For example: *"People who influenced teenager's attendance in this program included: Friends (22), Parents (14), Teachers (6), Coaches (3), Other (3)."*

## Percentage

When we want to show a relative weighting of some aspect of our data, calculating the percentage of a particular response in relation to other responses is helpful.

For example: *"Seventy-two percent of participating physicians report that they attend the conference primarily for networking."*

## Range

Occasionally, we simple want to see the full array of responses on an open-ended question.

For example: *"Program participants suggest the following ideas for improving the program: etc.)"How would you rate your life?"*

## Quantitative Technical Note D

### Thorny Issues

There are a number of thorny issues that we commonly experience as we engage quantitative evaluations. Here are a few to keep in mind:

#### Response rates

As you might imagine, your findings are valid only insofar as your sample is substantial and representative. The advantage you have over a classic survey researcher is that you have a captive audience; most researchers do not. Whenever possible, include all participants in your evaluation. When you can't, seek advice from someone who understands the technical nature of sample size and significance to help you.

Within a questionnaire, there is often an occasional nonresponse to a particular answer. If item nonresponse is less than 5% on any given item, you can assume that your mean or median will be sufficient. If it's more, do some research or talk to a researcher about what to do.

In order to increase the likelihood that you'll get a good response rate, build evaluation into the program. Carve out some time. Help it to be a learning and reflective experience for the participant. Have everyone do it together. Whatever you do, don't hand a questionnaire to people as they are heading to a meal, or to a car to leave, or on their way out the door after a long day.

#### Outliers

These are sub-groups of respondents or individuals who, for one reason or another, will have extreme and non-representative responses. Of course, you can't simply toss data because you don't like them. You have to care for the data somehow. (Occasionally, you'll find some of your best insights in outlier data.) If the data represent a substantial faction of respondents, then you'll need to work with it through means or medians. If it is a one-off (or something of the sort), you may extricate it from the data set, but you must still report it. Be very careful. Retain transparency and intellectual honesty as you report the outlier, including why you think the data may be so.

### Causality vs. Correlation

Unless you are performing a highly technical experiment, you'll have to be careful in claiming causality. Just because numbers change over the course of your intervention does not necessarily mean that the intervention caused the change. An accompanying qualitative portion to your evaluation will help you here. At least you will know, then, more about what participants are attributing as causing their growth and development.

### Hawthorne effect

In the late 1920s at a factory called Hawthorne Works, workers were studied to determine which intervention made them more productive. What researchers realized in time, however, was that the mere presence of research attention produced variance more than any intervention. This is a Hawthorne effect. Keep an eye on it. Sometimes people perform better simply because someone is watching.

### John Henry effect

Early in the days of the railroad automation, when rail lines like sinews crossed the American West, a rail-layer named John Henry tried to race an experimental technology to save his profession. He outperformed his normal effort to compete with the intervention. Keep an eye on this tendency in people to respond to competition instead of intervention.

## Quantitative Technical Note E

The confidences we may have in the power of the findings depend on our ability to defend the validity and reliability of the inquiry. Here are a couple of ideas to keep in mind:

### Validity

There are at least three kinds of validity to employ:

1. **Construct Validity.** Do the indicators you have chosen to measure actually relate to your core mission and ideas of essential impact?

2. **Content Validity.** Does someone else who is knowledgeable (a colleague or expert agree that your items represent the key ideas of E1-Activity and E3-Impact and will make sense to your respondents?

3. **Face Validity.** Do those who will be taking the test or other technically untrained readers, agree that the questions "look valid" and make sense to them?

### Reliability

Reliability refers to the dependability of the data. You won't be able to rely on it if your respondents are rushing, or hungry, or annoyed, or exhausted, or distracted, or even on an emotional high. Picture how the administration of a questionnaire when people are heading out the door after a long day, or right after there has been some intense emotional or relational high, or in the immediate wake of a substantial set-back, will make data unreliable. Pay attention to the factors that might compromise the dependability of your data. Try to protect the integrity of the evaluation. Poor data make poor findings.

**How to increase your confidence**

1. **Develop clear ideas about intended impact.** The work you put into clarifying your outcomes will prove to be extraordinarily helpful.c First you need to know what you want to achieve before you can design a valid quantitative instrument to measure it.

2. **Identify the most critical indicators of program execution (E1) and program impact (E3).** It's tempting to gather data simply because you can. Be sure to think through the direct indicators and outcomes of your work and limit your questionnaire design to those primary elements.

3. **Vet the items of your questionnaire with colleagues and experts.** Others will be able to provide perspective on the emphases and tenor of your questionnaire. Be sure to get a few qualified people to check the content validity of your instrument.

4. **Pilot the questionnaire.** Try it out on a few people from your target population and then revise. It requires multiple iterations to develop an effective instrument.

# Part 5

**Evaluation Strategy**

# Introduction to Evaluation Strategy

Let's put it all together now.

If we don't, we'll be left with a morass of protocols and instruments and no unifying approach to guide us. There will only be tasks. And tasks without meaning quickly become tiresome.

Our aim is to design an evaluation strategy that is simple and elegant, that can be joined by all of our colleagues and staff members and then applied broadly. Our desire is also to create durable habits of reflection that will refresh, guide, and inspire everyone.

In this way, evaluation can be true leadership. It is not simply a perfunctory task or after-thought. It is essential to our thinking about strategy and engagement with people. It can form the hearts and minds of those who practice and hear about evaluation. It is a key strand to organizational DNA.

> Evaluation...
> can form hearts
> and minds

Since every organization grows in the direction of its most persistent inquiries, how we handle evaluation can make all the difference in what kind of organization we become and what kind of impact we leave on our world.

# Designing an Evaluation Strategy

Evaluation is inextricably tied to strategy.

How will you know what to evaluate unless you first know what you aim to achieve and how you intend to achieve it? And how will you truly know what you aim to achieve until you think through what impact looks like?

Evaluation, then, should not be relegated to a side office or a detached evaluation expert; it should be central to the thinking of the organization's key leaders and strategists. Its design should accompany the design of strategy right at the outset of any endeavor.

(Granted, there are times when an external evaluator can give you perspectives and credibility you need to prove and improve your effectiveness. But we are focusing primarily on the ongoing practice of evaluation within organizations in this discussion. There is tremendous developmental power to gaining internal capacity for performing quality program evaluation.)

> Evaluation is inextricably tied to strategy.

Also, in order for evaluation to truly impact a program or organization, it has to be embedded meaningfully in the leaders of the program or organization. Sometimes programs or organizations have a dedicated "evaluation officer" that does the work for everyone. But that arrangement robs everyone of experiencing the developmental power of evaluation. It also usually prevents findings and recommendations from making any difference on the ground because:

➤ people don't understand what they haven't interacted with,

➤ people don't value what they haven't helped to create, and

➤ people won't apply what hasn't engaged them.

This is how we can have stacks of data in a central office making no difference to decision-makers on the front lines.

If evaluation doesn't make sense to program directors and staff, it is usually good only to prove value to funders and constituency but not to improve the programs' effects.

An evaluation strategy, then, should look like this:

1. **Simple and elegant.** Keep the design as crisp and clear as possible.

2. **Participatory.** Include a wide range of key leaders in the development and design of the strategy. Evaluation is usually more powerful for change when it involves the collective effort of leadership and staff.

3. **Iterative.** Return to the plan on a regular basis to offer multiple generations of the strategy, each more sufficient than the one before.

4. **Balanced.** Engage each of the E1-E4 quadrants.

5. **Strategic.** Positioned to affect the future direction of program design and capacity building.

Prepare a document that outlines primary evaluation questions, protocols and instruments, personnel responsible, timeline, and other logistics. Try your hand at designing a plan for evaluation.

## Worksheet 5.1

**Quantitative**

| Design | E1 Indicators | E3 Indicators | Personnel | Timeline |
|---|---|---|---|---|
| Instruments | | | | |

**Qualitative**

| Design | E2 Indicators | E4 Indicators | Personnel | Timeline |
|---|---|---|---|---|
| Population | | | | |
| Sample | | | | |
| Protocol | | | | |
| Individual interviews | | | | |
| Group Interviews | | | | |
| Observations | | | | |

# Creating a Culture of Evaluation

If evaluation becomes a durable habit—an ongoing practice that is embedded in the life of your team and organization—it can have a profound and positive effect.

Sometimes we do evaluation primarily to meet a deadline for a funder, accreditation review, or annual report to stakeholders. We exert herculean effort to gather data and get a report out the door. And the process, as well as the findings, affects us very little. We're simply relieved when it's over.

But if we embed evaluation in our ongoing habits of work, it can profoundly enrich our organizational culture and effectiveness. Here are some changes it can cause:

Shift from metrics to meaning.

> People long to attach their lives to meaning and purpose. The work of evaluation design and implementation can clarify deeper aims and re-awaken a passion within them to promote human growth and development.

Shift from cherished theories to evidence-based theories.

> We all have ideas about how people best change and grow.

Some of those theories are spot-on; others are simply groundless, legends in our own minds. Evaluation tends to re-engineer our thinking to gain better scientific precision and rely on evidence to inform our work.

**Shift from a focus on activity to focus on impact.**
Over time, people tend to fill their view with activity. We are all so busy. Our daily list of to-do can overwhelm us. Evaluation keeps us thinking about impact, not just activity, and lifts our gaze to a better horizon of human effect.

**Shift from a culture of assumptions to a culture of curiosity.**
Strategy is often formed by anecdotes and personal experiences. Evaluation makes us apply a disciplined curiosity about processes of human change instead.

**Shift from doing things to people to engaging with people.**
We fill our time talking about what we are going to do, when and to whom. Evaluation gets us close to people. It keeps us interacting with the people we are serving, seeking to understand them and their growth and development better.

**Shift from isolated work to collective work.**
Individuals, teams, and departments tend to work more independently and in greater isolation over time. A collective strategy for evaluation breaks down the silos and helps people gain a collective vision of impact.

**Shift from temporal focus to durable and cumulative impact.**
Whichever project is in front of us tends to consume our attention. But a good strategy for evaluation keeps our eyes focused on the broader and longer-term horizon of human effect.

## Worksheet 5.2

What is your vision for the impact of evaluation on you, your team, and your organization?

How might you take the next steps to develop your capacity through evaluation in service to your mission?

**Notes**

NOTES

NOTES

NOTES